DRUGS AND SUICIDE

People who think about suicide often feel helpless in their lives.

DRUGS AND SUICIDE

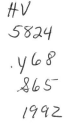

Judie Smith

THE ROSEN PUBLISHING GROUP, INC.

NEW YORK

The people pictured in this book are only models; they, in no way, practice or endorse the activities illustrated. Captions serve only to explain the subjects of photographs and do not in any way imply a connection between the real-life models and the staged situations.

Published in 1992 by The Rosen Publishing Group, Inc.
29 East 21st Street, New York, NY 10010

Copyright ©1992 by The Rosen Publishing Group, Inc.

First Edition

Printed in the United States of America.

Library of Congress Cataloging-in-Publication Data

Smith, Judie
  Drugs and suicide
  (The Drug abuse prevention library)
  Includes bibliographical references and index.
  Summary: Discusses drugs and suicide, how they can
  both function as forms of escape, how one can lead to
  another, and what the alternatives are.
     ISBN 0-8239-1421-6
     1. Teenagers—United States–Drug use—Juvenile
     literature. 2. Teenagers—United States—Suicidal
     behavior—Juvenile literature. [1. Drug abuse. 2.
     Suicide.] I. Title. II. Series.
     HV5824. Y68S65   1992
     362.2'0973—dc20   92-7962
                     CIP
                     AC

Contents

Strong feelings of loneliness make life seem worthless.

CHAPTER 1

About Suicide: A Tragic Way Out

*H*istory tells us many stories of people destroying each other in war. Warriors are the heroes of legends. We try to imagine the courage, strength, and wisdom it must take to become a hero. But history also describes how people have died because their lives became unbearable. They chose to kill themselves rather than suffer hurt and pain. They chose to die rather than be forced to serve an evil leader. At times, these suicide victims were thought of as heroes. But in other times, these victims were called cowards or even criminals. Different cultures and religions have had different ideas about suicide. Even in our

8 own country, these attitudes have changed over time.

Sometimes the stories about suicide are romantic, like *Romeo and Juliet*. Romeo and Juliet were only 14 years old. They fell in love, but their families would not permit them to see each other. Both lovers killed themselves when they thought the other had died. Shakespeare wrote this famous story to show us how tragic life can be. If the story could be rewritten, the parents might have understood how much their children loved each other. A death by suicide is not really romantic.

Suicide in Religion

Primitive people often made suicide part of religious ceremonies. Sometimes they even encouraged members of the tribe to kill themselves after a chief had died.

Until recently, it was customary in parts of India for a widow to kill herself after her husband died. If she did that, it would be easier for him to enter the next life. *Hara-kiri* (suicide) was also an honorable death for the nobles and warriors of Japan. And during World War II, Japanese fighter pilots crashed their planes into American ships. This made it difficult for Americans to defend themselves .

Other cultures have not viewed suicide as courageous or honorable. Most of the wise men of ancient Greece thought that suicide was cowardly. During the Middle Ages, people were taught that suicide was a sin against God, a most unholy act. A suicide victim could not be buried in a Christian cemetery.

Changing Ideas

The laws about suicide have changed in recent decades. Although it is still against the law to help someone else commit suicide, many people have debated the question of *euthanasia*. Euthanasia means ending someone else's life who is suffering or in great pain.

Some people still believe that suicide is a sin or a shameful act. Many others look at it as an escape from a long, painful life. There is the question when, if ever, people should be allowed to kill themselves with the help of a doctor. If they are very ill and have no hope of recovery, should they be permitted to die? Can a loving wife give an overdose of drugs to a husband who is dying of cancer?

Suicide is not the only way to end suffering. We need to encourage those who are suffering to find help.

10 *Some Things to Know About Suicide*

Three times as many teenagers are killing themselves now as in the 1950s. Suicide is one of North America's leading causes of death for teenagers. Only accidents cause more deaths each year. That means more young people die by suicide than from almost any other cause.

Boys commit suicide three to five times as often as girls. Boys use guns or other violent means, such as hanging. Girls prefer taking an overdose of drugs or slashing their wrists. They are not as likely to die with these methods. When a girl attempts suicide and dies, she has probably used a gun.

It is interesting that many more girls than boys attempt suicide and don't die. A suicide attempt is a way of asking for help. Girls seem to be more comfortable asking for help. It is a message that things are going badly and the person wants life to be different. Boys, on the other hand, usually want to solve their own problems. They find it hard to tell others of their pain.

It is estimated that one out of every ten teenagers does something to harm himself or herself deliberately. The parents may never even know about it.

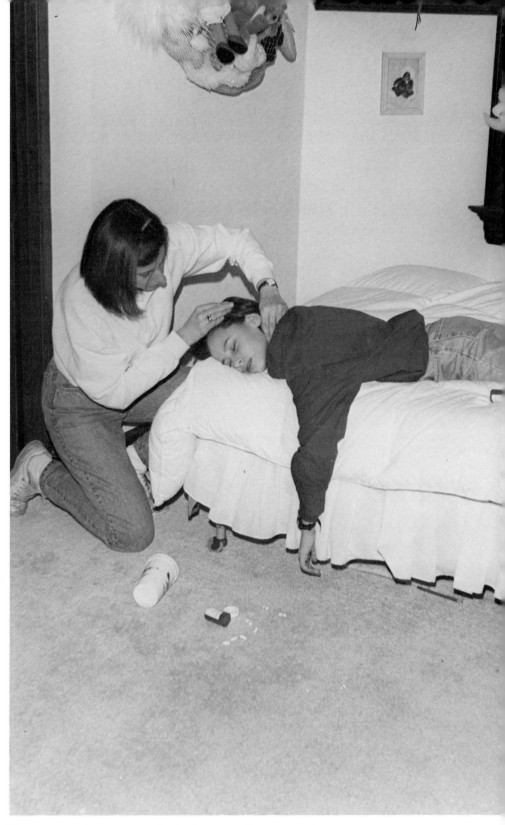

Many teens who attempt suicide do not really want to die.

12 *When Ben and his girlfriend, Shirley, had an argument, he told her he was going to kill himself. He went home to get his dad's hunting shotgun. When he got back to Shirley's house, he shouted to her to come outside to watch. Then he pulled the trigger. His mother never knew that he had tried to kill himself once before by driving his car into a tree. She thought it was an accident. But Shirley knew that he had done it on purpose. He had asked her never to tell anyone, and she didn't.*

Those who could have helped Ben never knew of his suicide attempt. It is believed that for every teenager who actually dies by suicide, at least a hundred others have also tried to kill themselves.

Maybe one out of every two young people considers suicide as a way to solve a serious problem. Having so many strong feelings such as fear, sadness, and anger, the person in crisis has trouble sorting through what will work best. It is not unusual to think about dying to make the sad or angry feelings go away.

When Sylvia found out that she was pregnant, she told her boyfriend. Wendel told her that in no way would he take responsibility. He wanted her to have an abortion. Sylvia did not want that. She couldn't sleep the night after talking to Wendel. She was afraid to tell her mother, who was already taking care of her sister's baby while her sister finished school. Sylvia looked at a bottle of sleeping pills in the medicine cabinet. She thought how easy it would be just to go to sleep and never wake up. But she finally decided instead to talk to her best friend the next day. She didn't want to kill her unborn child. There had to be another solution.

Not everyone who thinks about suicide actually does something dangerous. Most teens can find another way out of a crisis. They don't really want to die. They just want the hurt to go away.

Some Common Questions

As we have already seen, attitudes about suicide have changed in our society. Today we talk openly about suicide. That was not always true. Years ago if a suicide occurred, people tried to keep it a secret. Few scientists were interested in studying about it. No one knew how to help someone who was suicidal. But we now know that it is good to ask questions. Asking questions can help people like Sylvia.

A suicide threat may be a cry for help.

Let's look at some of the questions that people ask about suicide.

Question 1: If my friend talks about committing suicide, does it mean that he or she won't really do it?

Answer: No. You can't ever be sure of that. Often people who talk about suicide do attempt it or even complete the act. You might think that a friend talks about suicide to get attention. That may be true, but your friend may *need* some attention and may die trying to get it. Someone may also talk about suicide as a power play to gain control over others.

Sandy was 18 years old when she got married. She and her new husband had an argument on their wedding day. Vic said he might as well kill himself if that was how she was going to act. As the years went by, he continued to use the threat of suicide to control her. He bought a gun. Then he started pointing it at himself whenever they argued. Sandy gave in and gave in. One night, Vic put the loaded gun to his head and said he was going to kill himself. She was very angry, so she said, "Well, go ahead." He did. Whether he meant to or not, he took his own life.

16

Question 2: Does every person who attempts suicide want to die?

Answer: No. In fact, most people who attempt suicide do *not* want to die. It is the only way they can think of to make the pain go away, to get someone's attention, or get back at someone if they are angry. Sometimes a part of them wants to die and a part wants to live. It becomes a conflict inside them, and they may not even understand what is going on.

Tommy drove his car to the emergency room parking lot of a large hospital. He pulled into a spot close to the door where the guard could see him. Then Tommy shot himself. The part of him that wanted to die pulled the trigger. The part of him that wanted to live drove to the hospital first.

Question 3: If you think that someone is considering suicide, should you ask?

Answer: Yes. Don't worry about giving others the idea of suicide. You cannot cause others to kill themselves by asking whether they are thinking about it. If you see a friend doing things that may be warning signs of suicide, find out what is going on. Many people feel sad but would never kill themselves. Others may feel sad and really consider killing themselves.

A good friend can help a depressed person find counseling for a serious problem.

18 Since suicide is hard to discuss, people who are suicidal often have no one to talk to about it. Listening to a troubled friend's problems and letting him or her know that you understand is very helpful. Of course, if a friend does talk to you about suicide, you must always let someone else know.

Question 4: Does suicide often happen without warning?

Answer: Not often. Most of the time suicidal people leave clues to their plans. Remember, most people who attempt suicide usually do not want to die. They may not realize it, but they hope someone will notice how they are acting. They want someone to ask how they are feeling about the difficult situation they are facing. One of the clearest warning signs is a previous suicide attempt. Most young people who are suicidal usually try more than once. Because there are many warning signs, we know that suicides can be prevented. It is best for young people to learn to recognize those warning signs.

Question 5: Once a person is suicidal, is that person suicidal forever?

Answer: No. Persons who wish to kill themselves are suicidal for a short time. A crisis does not last forever. Problems do get solved. Depression can be treated.

That is why it is so important to put off a
decision to commit suicide when you are
feeling bad. It is quite possible to discover
ways to make the hard times better. Then
you may never think about suicide again.

Question 6: Is suicide inherited?

Answer: No. But once a suicide occurs
in a family, other members may be at risk.
That does not mean that being suicidal is
inherited. It only means that one victim's
suicide may make it seem that it is also all
right for other family members to go ahead
and kill themselves.

Much of our behavior is learned. Suicide
is an individual choice. It is not passed on
from one generation to the next. Even
though the tendency to commit suicide
appears in some families, it is not the
result of a hereditary trait.

Question 7: Are all suicidal people
insane?

Answer: Certainly not. A suicide
attempt may be made to try to solve a
crisis. The person may not be thinking
clearly when the attempt is made. But
that does not mean he or she is insane.
Many suicidal people do show signs of
depression and sadness. When a sad
person doesn't want to go to school or be
with friends and has no energy to do much

20 of anything for weeks at a time, it may be called a mental illness. However, not all suicidal people are depressed. And not all depressed people are suicidal.

Warning Signs

How can you tell if someone is suicidal? Eighty percent of all the young people who attempt suicide have given warning signs. Think about the clues that follow, and be aware of changes in your friends' behavior.

- **Talking about suicide.**

  Sara put herself under great pressure to excel in school. When she was caught cheating on an exam, Sara told her friend that it didn't matter to her anymore if she lived or died.

- **Giving away prized possessions.**

  Henry gave his boom box to his best friend. He also gave his lockermate his favorite gold chain. Henry said he wouldn't need those things where he was going.

- **Signs of depression.**

  Betty began to lose a lot of weight but claimed she wasn't on a diet. It always seemed as if she were about to cry.

- **Irritability, mood changes, impulsiveness.**

  Jim was sharp and edgy. His moods shifted quickly. One minute he seemed

Loss of appetite and energy may be signs of deep depression.

Many people who are considering suicide give away their most valued possessions to others.

dazed. The next minute he was picking a fight with someone.

- **Taking risks.**

  Paul began driving his car like a wild man. He had a minor accident and got two speeding tickets in one week. He laughed about it and said not to worry.

- **Loss of interest, withdrawal.**

  After Jenny's boyfriend broke up with her, she had a hard time paying attention in class. She quit taking piano lessons and dropped out of the church choir.

- **Low self-esteem.**

  Kitty didn't feel good about herself. Her dad kept telling her she wouldn't amount to anything, and she believed it.

- **Decline in grades.**

  Eric used to be a good student. He began to skip school. He flunked algebra and said it didn't matter. He said where he was going he wouldn't need math.

- **Preoccupation with death and dying.**

  Yolanda expressed herself by writing beautiful poetry. Her English teacher noticed that in recent weeks the repeated theme was death and lonely graveyards.

One or two of these signs alone may not mean that someone is thinking of suicide. Watch for several signs at once.

Over-the-counter drugs can become addictive if they are misused.

CHAPTER 2

About Drugs: The War Close to Home

*D*rugs are chemical substances that change the way the brain and other body systems work. Drugs also change the way we think and feel.

Some drugs are helpful and are used by doctors to cure illnesses. When a doctor understands what is causing a problem, he or she may write a prescription for certain medicine to help fight the illness. Prescription drugs should be taken only as the doctor orders.

Other drugs can be purchased in a drugstore without a doctor's prescription. They are called over-the-counter drugs. Cough medicine and aspirin are examples of over-the-counter drugs. When they are

25

26 used according to directions on the package, they also can be helpful. But when they are taken too frequently, they can be just as dangerous as illegal drugs.

Some of the common illegal drugs are marijuana, cocaine, and heroin. It is against the law to use these drugs or to have even a small amount of them in your possession.

"Legal" Drugs

Other drugs are legal for adults, but illegal for school-age children. These drugs include alcohol and tobacco products. It is against the law to sell liquor or beer to anyone who is under 21.

These drugs can do serious damage to a growing body. But there are other reasons to make them illegal. They are "gateway" drugs. Using them at an early age makes it more likely that you will go on to even more dangerous drugs. Using any drug as a teenager also means that you may start to become dependent on that drug.

Inhalants are another category of drugs. Commonly abused inhalants include glue, liquid white-out, paint thinner, spray paints, gasoline, and acrylic markers or pens. These products are sniffed and produce profound changes in the brain.

Many drugs alter judgment. People who are high on drugs may attempt to do dangerous things and cause serious accidents.

Drug Misuse and Abuse

28

Three terms are most commonly used to describe how drugs are used: *use, misuse,* and *abuse*. The United States Food and Drug Administration defines *drug use* as "taking a drug for its intended purpose, in the appropriate amount, frequency, strength, and manner." When you follow a doctor's orders you are using a drug appropriately.

Drug misuse is "taking a substance for its intended purpose, but not in the appropriate amount, frequency, strength, or manner." If the dentist prescribes a painkiller for your toothache, but you take more than is ordered, you are misusing it.

Drug abuse is "deliberately taking a substance for other than its intended purpose in a manner that can result in damage to the person's health or ability to function." Sniffing the fumes of spray paint is clearly abusing the intended purpose of a can of paint. There is no proper use for illegal drugs such as cocaine or LSD, or for alcohol by persons under the age of 21. Drug abuse may form a dangerous pattern that affects the behavior of the user.

Most teenagers try drugs and alcohol because they see others doing it.

Drug Use Through The Centuries

Ancient magicians and healers discovered the strange effects drugs had on the mind. Every culture has used alcohol in rituals once it learned to turn grapes into wine. Poppies produced opium in the Middle East. Coca grew wild in the jungles of South America. Doctors in Europe and America learned about Indian marijuana and some other painkillers from the early healers. Have you ever seen old movies about the West where "snake oil" salesmen sold "patent medicines"? These products contained drugs like heroin, morphine, and codeine. Even the original Coca-Cola soft drink contained cocaine. It became popular as a "pick-me-up."

Prohibition

Eventually, people came to realize how dangerous it was to use drugs that cause addiction and dependency. Coca-Cola stopped using cocaine in 1903. Laws were passed making it illegal for anyone except doctors to dispense these powerful drugs. From 1919 to 1933, alcoholic beverages were against the law. During this period, criminals made a lot of money by selling liquor. When the laws failed to stop people from drinking, they were repealed.

Avoiding drugs is the best way to avoid drug-related problems.

The Drug Decade

During the 1960s, attitudes changed once again. Students began to experiment with drugs like LSD and marijuana. New drugs were prescribed by doctors to ease tension and depression. People sometimes took tranquilizers instead of learning how to cope with day-to-day pressures.

Anabolic steroids became popular with professional and amateur athletes alike. The immediate effects of steroids are to strengthen muscles and give a feeling of confidence. The long-term effects include serious and sometimes fatal consequences.

In 1992, Lyle Alzado, one of the great defensive linemen of professional football, died while still in his forties. He himself blamed his illness on the frequent use of steroids during his playing years. The use of steroids is now forbidden in both amateur and professional athletics.

Cocaine reappeared in the 1970s. In the 1980s crack appeared on the scene.

The War on Drugs

The enormous problems that dangerous drugs caused young people and their families in the 1980s have led educators and parents to wage war against drug use. Drug use can lead to addiction. The law

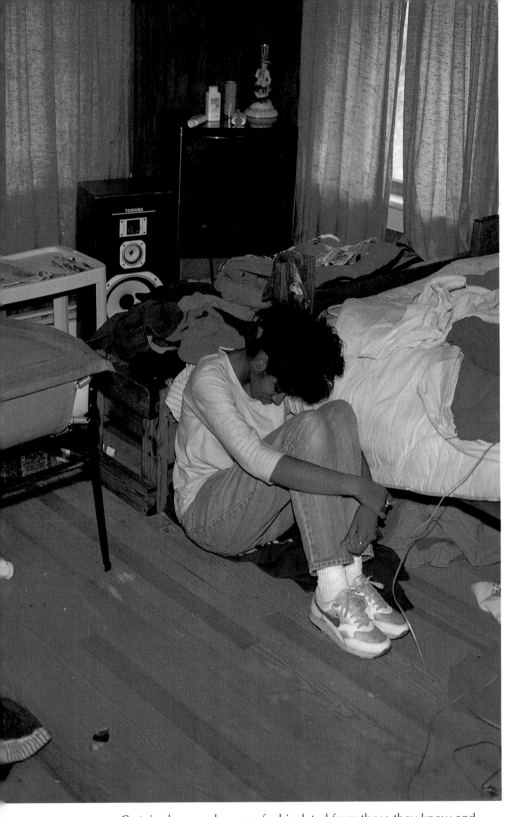

Certain drugs make users feel isolated from those they know and love, such as friends and family.

punishes those who are caught using or
selling illegal drugs. However, being sent
to prison or juvenile detention is minor
punishment compared to the effects drugs
have on the body and brain.

Cocaine and Crack

Cocaine was once thought to be a wonder
drug that would not cause addiction. We
now know that cocaine and crack can be
highly addictive.

Cocaine is injected or sniffed. Crack is
the street name for tiny chunks or "rocks"
of cocaine. It is smoked, and it makes a
crackling sound when it burns. Crack has
two specific effects on the body. It acts as
a stimulant and as a painkiller. Cocaine
narrows the blood vessels. It increases the
blood pressure, the heart and respiratory
rates, and the body temperature. It changes
the brain's electrical activity. The brain is
like a headquarters or control center. Its
nerve cells control all the systems of the
body. Cocaine use causes one nerve cell to
send electrical messages to the next cell
much too quickly. This stimulation
creates a sensation much like the scary
thrill of riding a roller coaster. This is
what cocaine users call a *rush*. Cocaine
also causes a *high* that is like an intense

34 sense of happiness. But that lasts only a matter of minutes. Then it turns into a lasting feeling of restlessness, irritability, and general depression.

Repeated use of cocaine interferes with the normal functioning of the brain's nerve cells. It takes ever-increasing amounts of cocaine to make the brain work the same way again. The body builds up a natural resistance to the effects of the drug. This tolerance to the drug causes users to become addicted. If they try to stop, the brain goes into *withdrawal*. Without more cocaine the person who is addicted then becomes depressed and is in physical pain. Continued use of cocaine can cause heart attacks, brain seizures, or mental illness. The effects of cocaine use vary greatly according to the individual. Nevertheless, it is safe to say that cocaine is an extremely dangerous drug.

When a pregnant woman regularly uses cocaine, her unborn child is affected. Her baby is at a much higher risk for retardation. It may have trouble with its eyes and brain. Many "cocaine or crack babies" are born with serious problems. They have to live through several weeks of very painful and often life-threatening withdrawal symptoms.

Marijuana 35

Marijuana is also called "pot," "weed," or "grass." The *cannabis* plant grows wild in most areas of the world that have a wet and warm climate. About a third of the U.S. supply of marijuana comes from Mexico. During the 1960s, marijuana was widely used by many young people who experimented with it as a recreational drug. It was commonly thought that pot was relatively harmless. But several things have changed people's attitude toward marijuana since then. A new type of marijuana is now grown in the United States. The new strain has a much higher concentration of the active chemical, THC. It is much more powerful and addictive than the kind grown in Mexico. Now the age of smokers for this new drug is getting younger and younger.

Smoking pot causes changes to the mind and body. Time and space become confused, causing distortion. Judgment, logic, and memory are almost always impaired. Continued heavy use can cause serious mental and emotional problems.

THC can remain in the body for as long as a week.

People are now well aware of the many dangers of cigarette smoke and how it can

36 damage the lungs and cause cancer. Smoking marijuana increases the risk of lung cancer even more than tobacco. One joint (rolled pot) irritates the lungs about as much as a whole pack of cigarettes.

Marijuana is not as highly addictive as other drugs, such as heroin. But regular marijuana users need larger amounts to obtain the same high. Long-time users have some physical problems when they try to stop. But it is possible for even weekend smokers to develop certain personality and character changes.

Alcohol

Alcohol is considered a drug because it changes the way you behave and feel. Alcohol is a more destructive drug than either cocaine or marijuana. It is not illegal for adults. In many places, alcohol is socially acceptable. For teenagers who are still maturing it can affect both their physical and emotional growth. Like tobacco, alcohol is a gateway drug. Those who abuse alcohol are more likely to go on to other illegal substances.

A small amount of alcohol acts as a stimulant. People drink socially to relax and enjoy themselves at parties. However, even a small amount of alcohol changes

Drug and alcohol addiction takes hold faster in youngsters and teens than in adults.

38 judgment and reaction time. Sixty percent of all automobile accident deaths each year are connected with drinking.

A moderate amount of alcohol acts as a depressant just like a sleeping pill. The brain and body systems slow down, and other personality changes occur. All too often someone under the influence of alcohol becomes aggressive and abusive. Fights and child abuse are often attributed to drunkenness. Large quantities of alcohol can cause respiratory failure and death.

Jerry was a freshman at a large and respected university. He joined a popular fraternity. The fraternity members put the pledges through traditional initiation ceremonies. Jerry was blindfolded and given several six-packs of beer in the back of a pickup truck. He was told to drink them quickly. He passed out before they reached the heavily wooded area. Once there, he was left alone in the middle of the night. When he did not return to the fraternity house the next day, the members drove back to the woods and found him dead, lying just where they left him. He had died of acute alcohol poisoning.

One 12-ounce can of beer, one 5-ounce glass of wine, and one ½-ounce glass of

liquor all contain the same amount of
alcohol. You can get drunk from each just
as quickly. There is no quick way to sober
up. Black coffee or a cold shower does not
improve the blurred vision, the severe
lack of coordination, or the disorientation
of drunkenness. Only time helps to get
sober. After the body rids itself of the
drug it may still suffer the unpleasant
after-effect of a hangover. Vomiting and
headaches may last into the following day.

The heavy use of alcohol eventually
leads to dependence and addiction. When
an alcoholic tries to stop drinking all at
once, he or she is likely to suffer severe
and dangerous withdrawal symptoms
called delirium tremens or "DTs." These
can include convulsions, fears, and even
hallucinations (seeing things that are not
really there). Continued heavy drinking
leads to poor health and permanent
physical damage.

Danger to an Unborn Baby

As with many other drugs, if a woman
abuses alcohol during pregnancy, her
unborn baby may be affected. This effect
is called "fetal alcohol syndrome." Such
babies are born smaller and grow more
slowly than normal babies. They may

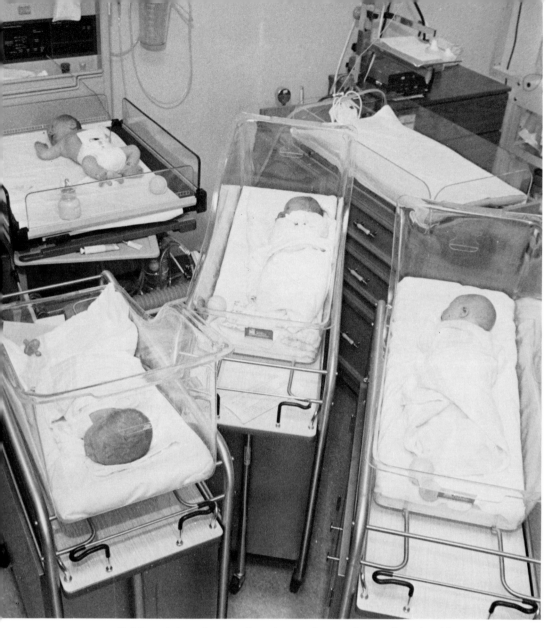

Babies of drug-free mothers have a better chance for a healthy start in life.

have learning difficulties and other behavior problems when they enter school. To be extra safe, pregnant mothers should avoid any kind of drug, including even a small amount of alcohol.

Inhalants

Sniffing the fumes of various common products such as aerosol paint or even gasoline can produce effects that are more serious than any of the other drugs. Glue, paint thinner, and liquid white-out are easily available to young people. Most states now restrict their purchase by minors. The inhaled vapors reach the brain quickly and cause disorientation, lack of coordination, and impaired judgment. If the vapors are inhaled deeply, or a large amount is used over a short period of time, the user is in danger of severe brain damage or death. Repeated sniffing can result in fatigue, loss of appetite, nausea, sneezing, nosebleeds, headaches, and permanent damage to the nervous system.

The Scope of the Problem

Research studies report that younger and younger students are becoming involved with drugs. Fourth-graders are beginning to experiment with illegal substances. The regular use of tobacco often starts at that age, too. By the time they reach fifth and sixth grade, 17 percent have tried alcohol and 2 percent have already experimented with marijuana. According to the U.S.

42 Department of Education, one quarter of high-school graduates are frequent users of illegal drugs. Two thirds of these are frequent users of alcohol, and one fifth smoke tobacco daily. Over 50 percent have used marijuana, over 10 percent have tried hallucinogens such as LSD and PCP, and over 90 percent have used alcoholic beverages.

Symptoms of Drug Abuse

When drugs or alcohol become an escape, a young person's behavior may change. The following are warning signals of abuse.

- **Loss of interest in usual activities.**

  Max worked hard to make the soccer team. He attended all practices and worked out. But halfway through the season Max began skipping practice. Then he quit the team and told the coach that he just didn't have time for sports.

- **Physical symptoms.**

  Glassy, bloodshot eyes, enlarged pupils, wearing of dark glasses, staggering or stumbling, slurred speech, constant fatigue, injuries, frequent colds, coughing, runny nose, vomiting, and weight loss.

  Max often went to the school clinic. The nurse noticed his red eyes and runny nose and asked if he had any allergies.

- **Mood changes.**

Max used to be well liked and respected by his teachers. Then he became quiet, negative, and quick-tempered.

Even with his classmates, Max became guarded and private. At home, he spent most of the time in his room.

- **Changes in friends.**

Many of Max's old friends noticed that he hung around with a group who were known to get into trouble and drink a lot. He did not take any of them home.

- **Lack of interest, decline in grades.**

Max had been a steady, above average student. With the other changes in his behavior he also let his studies go. He received three failing notices.

- **Frequent lies, broken promises.**

Max's mother asked for help from the school counselor when Max stayed out all night and then told her he had fallen asleep at a friend's house. When they met for a parent conference she also disclosed that money was missing from her purse.

The counselor met with Max's coach and teacher. The pattern of altered behaviors became clear. The school recommended that Max have a chemical assessment by a drug counselor to see how involved he was with drugs.

Many drugs alter reality and may lead to suicidal behavior.

CHAPTER 3

Escape Through Drugs and Suicide

*U*nfortunately, drugs and suicide often go hand in hand. Drug and alcohol abuse are considered by some to be slow forms of suicide. Nearly 6 out of 10 teenagers who commit suicide have abused drugs, and many also drink alcohol heavily. Their ability to deal with life disappears when they rely on drugs to avoid tough situations. Over 15 percent of all known alcoholics eventually die by suicide.

False Solution

Drugs give adolescents a temporary and false sense of security in dealing with their problems. They think of themselves as stronger, smarter, and more capable when they are stoned or drunk.

46   Many adolescents who commit suicide have used drugs or alcohol shortly before their death. A large amount of alcohol or drugs may reduce the fear of death. Fear of death may keep a person alive until the crisis passes and the problem is solved. Without the fear, the person may have a false sense of courage.

Reasons to Live

Fear of dying and other thoughts usually prevent suicidal teenagers from actually harming themselves. Perhaps they don't want to hurt their parents. Maybe they believe in a loving God who will take care of them. Or perhaps they fear that their soul will not go to heaven if they take their own life. Maybe they have hope that the sadness and anger will disappear if they just hang in there. Many more young people think of killing themselves than really act on the thought.

Young people have a tendency to do things quickly without thinking about the consequences. When a teenager has been drinking, sniffing, or using drugs, he or she is more likely to act impulsively. The influence of drugs and liquor makes it easier to express anger and unhappiness through suicidal behavior.

Means of Escape

Use of drugs may be an escape from feelings. Intense feelings can hurt as much as any physical pain. Anger is red-hot. Fear is icy cold and sends chills throughout the body. Sadness is so heavy that it becomes difficult to move. Feeling bad makes it hard to think.

When Maria thought that her sister would send her back to Mexico to live with an aunt, she was overwhelmed with panic. It would mean giving up her dream of becoming an American citizen. Most of all, it would separate her from José. She had met her boyfriend in high school.

One Saturday, Maria was invited to go to a party with José. Maria drank a lot of beer with the other young people and didn't come home until after 3:00 A.M. Her sister and brother-in-law were furious. The family decided that Maria would be better off away from the freedoms that American teens had. Maria ran away. She was found two days later in a shelter for runaways. She was drunk and had cut her wrists severely.

It is unlikely that Maria would have tried to commit suicide if she had not been drinking heavily. Alcohol had allowed her suicidal impulse to become stronger.

48 | *Conformity*

Teenagers want to be like their friends. They dress alike, listen to the same music, and use the same slang. A fifth-grade teacher could not understand why her students came to class with their shoelaces untied. She was concerned that they would trip, and kept reminding them to tie them. Finally someone explained that tying laces was considered "uncool."

When young people offer others a spray paint can to sniff, a joint to smoke, or a hit of coke, it could be a sign of friendship. An invitation to join the others in a group means being accepted. Being one of the group means trying to be like them.

A certain status and admiration for one another come from sharing drugs. An artificial sense of satisfaction may follow. Being one of a group means not being alone. One of the greatest sources of unhappiness for teens is being a loner or an outsider. That lonely feeling of being unconnected is sometimes the major reason for young people to start using drugs or drinking. Being drunk or stoned is only a temporary escape from loneliness. When the drug wears off, the user has a heightened feeling of loneliness.

Being part of a positive peer group can help teens keep their lives on track.

When Life Gets Tough

50 Is childhood really a wonderful, carefree
period of life? Childhood should be a time
to play, learn, and grow up surrounded by
a loving family. Yet, the world young
people live in today is not always a safe,
happy place. Pressures, dangers, and
conflicts are found in schools, homes, and
neighborhoods. It seems that children
today face many more problems and
dangerous situations than in the past.
They have to make important choices
before they really have the maturity to do
so. Some have to learn to make those
choices and manage their problems alone.
They have no responsible adult in their life
to guide them through difficult times.
Other homes have parents who do not
know how to listen to their children's
problems. Or the parents are facing their
own struggles and have no time or energy
to spare for their children.

Most young people are able to learn to
solve problems. They can ask for help
when they need it. And they can become
interested in healthy activities like sports
and avoid peers who use drugs or get into
trouble with the law. They are motivated
to do well in their classes and to graduate

from high school.   Most children grow up **51**
in homes that have strong values. They
learn to respect others, to be loving, and to
feel good about themselves.

Spread of Violence

For others, life is not so easy or safe.
Violence has spilled from the streets into
the school buildings. Some schools lock
all but one entrance in order to keep out
any troublemakers. Other schools have
installed metal detectors to keep students
from bringing in weapons. Students are
afraid of the fights that go on between
rival gangs. Parents forbid their children
to walk home alone. Some inner-city
neighborhoods are so dangerous that even
the criminals are afraid after dark.

Family Problems

Problems also occur outside the big cities.
The reported incidence of child abuse is
higher than ever. Divorce continues to
split families. Many children are born to
teenage mothers who have little means of
support. In other homes, both parents
must work and children are unsupervised
after school. These problems can also
exist in small towns and in the suburbs.

52 These are only a few of the more obvious problems that young people face today. Stress and pressure can come from many sources. Can you keep up your grades and be accepted to the college of your choice? Were you cut from the school football team? Did you finally make the cheerleading squad? Will our country go to war? How do you manage when your boyfriend wants to break up? What do you do when someone makes a racial slur? What do you do when your friends want you to join them in a beer or a joint?

Illegal drugs are readily available in small towns and rural areas. The whole nation is involved in preventing young people from using illegal drugs. Who has not heard of the "Just Say No" campaign? Drugs can be an escape when life gets tough. However, drugs only make the problems worse.

Addiction and Dependency

If drug use continues, addiction follows. No one starts taking drugs believing that the drugs will really control his or her life. But the body eventually needs more and more of the drug to get a high. Eventually, more and more is needed just to stop the pain and there is no longer a high. Obtaining the drug becomes more important than eating or keeping safe.

"It Runs in the Family"

Anyone who takes drugs like cocaine long enough will become addicted. However, some people have a tendency to abuse drugs and alcohol. Such people seem to have a biologically lower tolerance level. Once drug use begins, it is more difficult to stop. There is some evidence that this tendency to addiction may be inherited. Family history may reveal that a dependency is passed on in a family through the genes. For an example, if both of your parents are alcoholics, you are 400 times more likely to become addicted to alcohol or another drug than those whose parents are not alcoholics.

Addiction does not provide an escape from frustrating life situations. The many problems created are soon worse than any possible gain. Nothing is more disturbing than severe loneliness and depression. Negative attitudes and lower self-esteem often occur with drug use, leading to still greater despair. Using drugs to escape makes life even tougher.

Discussing problems with a parent or counselor can help make life's problems seem less troubling.

CHAPTER 4

Alternatives to Drugs and Suicide

*I*n many ways, the same things that stop kids from turning to drugs prevent them from attempting suicide. Both drugs and suicide are self-destructive. They are choices someone makes. Both of these dangers are preventable.

Developing Positive Qualities

Let's look at some of the positive qualities you need to develop as you grow up.

• **High self-esteem.** It takes a lot of confidence in oneself to be able to say no to drugs. Drugs may be a way to become accepted by a group of peers. Becoming part of a social group is important for adolescents. Being isolated during those

55

56 years can hurt. You need to become motivated and seek positive activities that bring satisfaction.

• **Social skills.** Social skills help people make friends. Young people who know how to keep friends feel socially accepted.

• **Communication skills.** Learning to express thoughts and feelings and to listen to what others have to say should be part of growing up.

Lines of communication should be kept open with your parents. Both drugs and suicide need to be talked about at home.

• **Knowing how to fail.** Much can be learned from failure. You learn that you can survive. You can learn that it is okay not to be perfect, and that making a mistake does not make you a bad person. Failure also teaches how to deal with losses. Most teenagers who are suicidal are suffering from some kind of loss or the shame of a failure.

• **A sense of responsibility.** Responsibility means learning the effect of your behavior. It also means carefully considering whether your actions are proper or not. Eventually self-control grows out of responsibility.

Enabling

Enabling is any behavior that makes it easier for a teenager to continue addictive behavior. If friends or family or teachers do nothing to stop drug or alcohol abuse, they become "enablers."

Some ways people "enable" others in drug or alcohol abuse are:

1. Keeping secrets. Sharing personal things with a buddy is part of friendship. But, when it comes to substance abuse, let parents or counselors know that someone you know has a problem.

2. Avoiding finding out when you are suspicious. If there is anything to be curious about, ask.

3. Ignoring a problem makes you part of the problem. Be willing to get involved. Try to be part of the solution.

4. Denying. Refusing to believe the evidence that drugs and alcohol are becoming a problem. Try to admit to yourself that something is troubling your drug- or alcohol-dependent friend.

5. Making excuses. Telling others that it is just a way of blowing off steam or having fun. Don't cover up the seriousness of your friend's dependency.

58 *Suicide: What Doesn't Help*

Scaring or arguing will not prevent a drug user who is in a crisis from attempting suicide. People decide to kill themselves because of the intense emotional pain they are experiencing. Reducing the pain will help to change their mind. Scaring them only adds unnecessary fear.

Never try to make someone who is suicidal feel guilty. Don't ask if he or she has given thought to how much grief suicide would cause family and friends. Don't say that suicide is a sin. Someone in a crisis is, in a sense, very selfish. The pain he or she is feeling is so great that nothing else seems more important.

Never dare or tease a suicidal friend. A freshman at college took his life after his girlfriend told him he didn't have the guts to commit suicide. When he begged her and threatened to kill himself, she thought he was trying to control her. The suicide that followed was a tragedy.

One last thing to avoid when someone you know is talking about suicide is giving advice. Trying to solve someone else's problems seldom works. When someone is feeling suicidal, telling the person what to do only adds to his or her feeling of helplessness.

Help List

Telephone Book

Yellow Pages
Drug Abuse, Counseling, Social Service Organizations

White Pages
Community Services, Hot Line for suicide prevention or drug abuse

School
Counselors, school nurse, Drug Education and Student Services, Health Services

Community
Church
YMCA
YWCA

Places That Have Support Groups
Your city's National Council on Alcoholism
County mental health services
County juvenile services
Your school counseling office
Your school nurse
Teen clinic

Places You Can Call or Write:

The Suicide Prevention Center
1041 South Menlo Ave.
Los Angeles, CA 90006
(213) 386-5111
or call your local Hot Line number for help and information

The American Association of Suicidology
2459 South Ash
Denver, CO 80222
(303) 692-0985

National Center for Death Education
New England Institute of Applied Arts and Sciences
656 Beacon St.
Boston, MA 02215
(617) 536-6970

Narcotics Anonymous
World Service Office
16155 Wyandotte St.
Van Nuys, CA 91406

Toughlove
P.O. Box 1069
Doylestown, PA 18901

Check the bulletin boards in the school nurse's office and counseling office for the TEEN HOT LINES in your town.

Glossary—
Explaining New Words

addiction Irresistible compulsion to use a drug in increasing dose and frequency.

apathy Lack of feeling, indifference.

attitude One's position on or feeling about a certain subject.

behavior of concern Unusual behavior or changes in behavior that indicate problems.

chemical assessment Assessment of level of drug abuse.

conformity Being like others.

delirium tremens (DTs) Uncomfortable condition caused by the sudden withdrawal from drugs.

dependency Need for a certain drug in order to function normally.

depressant Drug that reduces the working of the central nervous system.

depression Prolonged and severe feelings of sadness.

drug A chemical substance that changes the way the brain and other body systems normally work.

drug abuse Deliberate use of a drug for other than its intended purpose which can result in damage to health or ability to function. Drug abuse is also use of illegal drugs and alcohol by minors.

drug misuse Taking a substance for its intended purpose but not in the appropriate amount or frequency.

drug use Taking a drug for its intended purpose in the appropriate amount, frequency, and strength.

enabling Acting in ways that make it easier for someone to continue addictive behavior.

gateway drug Less harmful drug that leads to use of more dangerous drugs.

hallucinogen Drug that produces great changes in seeing and feeling.

inhalant Chemical that gives off mind-altering vapors or fumes.

inherit To receive a trait from an ancestor through genes.

preoccupation State of being lost in thought.

stimulant Drug that reverses mental and physical fatigue.

suicide Intentional ending of one's life.

tolerance Need for increased drug dosage to produce the same effect.

For Further Reading

About Teens and Drugs. South Deerfield, MA: Channing L. Bete Co., 1987.

Crook, Marion. *Teenagers Talk about Suicide*. Toronto: NC Press Limited, 1989.

DeVault, Christine, and Strong, Bryan. *Christy's Chance*. Santa Cruz, CA: Network Publications, 1987.

Don't Lose a Friend to Drugs. Washington, DC: National Crime Prevention Council, 1986.

Gordon, Sol. *When Living Hurts*. New York: Bantam Doubleday Dell Publishing Group, Inc., 1988.

Kolehmainen, Janet, and Handwerk, Sandra. *Teen Suicide*. Minneapolis: Lerner Publications, 1986.

Newton, Miller. *Gone Way Down: Teenage Drug Use Is a Disease*. Tampa: American Studies Press, 1987.

Smith, Judie. *Coping with Suicide*. New York: Rosen Publishing Group, 1990.

Index

About the Author

Judie Smith is a crisis specialist for the Psychological/ Social Services Department of the Dallas Independent School District. She works with children and their families who experience life crisis situations and helps schools recover from the aftermath of traumatic events.

Ms. Smith received an MA degree in Child Development and Welfare from the University of Minnesota and a BA in Psychology from DePauw University.

She has written two books, *Coping with Suicide* and *Suicide Prevention: A Crisis Intervention Curriculum for Teenagers and Young Adults;* and has coauthored the *Curriculum Standards on Suicide* for the National School Safety Council and *Postvention Guidelines* for The American Association of Suicidology.

Photo Credits
Cover: Stuart Rabinowitz
Photo on page 40, Stephanie FitzGerald; page 49, Dru Nadler; all other photos by Stuart Rabinowitz

Design and Production: Blackbirch Graphics, Inc.